Light
IN THE DARKNESS

25 Devotionals for Trauma Survivors

Charlotte B. Thomason

Houston, TX

Light in the Darkness Copyright © 2022 Charlotte B. Thomason.

No part of this book may be reproduced or transmitted in any form or by any mean, electronic or mechanical, including photocopying and recording, or by any information storage or retrieval system, except as may be expressly permitted in writing by the author. Requests for permission should be addressed in writing to:
Charlotte B. Thomason
charlotte@charlottethomason.com

Scripture quotations are from the ESV® Bible (The Holy Bible, English Standard Version®), copyright © 2001 by Crossway, a publishing ministry of Good News Publishers. Used by permission. All rights reserved.

Published 2022 by Plumb Line Press, Houston, TX.
Cover design and book layout by Legacy Marketing Services.

Print: 978-1-953279-23-1
Digital: 978-1-953279-24-8

LCCN: 2022949659

Plumb Line Press
Houston, TX

An imprint of Efusion Media Group
www.efusionmg.com

Table of Contents

A Note from the Author 2

How to Use This Devotional 3

Week 1: Hope 4

    Day One: A New Thing 5

    Day Two: Keeper of your Soul 8

    Day Three: Patience in the Gap 11

    Day Four: The Hidden Things 14

    Day Five: Hope in Him 17

    Day Six: I Hope in your Word 20

    Weekly Reflection 23

    Weekly Renewal 24

Week 2: Love 25

    Day One: The Gift 27

    Day Two: First Love 30

    Day Three: In this is Love 33

Day Four: God So Loved Us 36

Day Five: His Steadfast Love 39

Day Six: Write it on your Heart 42

Weekly Reflection 45

Weekly Renewal 46

Week 3: Peace 47

Day One: No Fear 49

Day Two: Peace Beyond Measure 52

Day Three: Peaceful Sleep 55

Day Four: Peace for the Nations• 58

Day Five: Blessed 61

Day Six: Perfect Peace 64

Weekly Reflection 67

Weekly Renewal 68

Week 4: Joy 69

Day One: Rejoice, Pray, Give Thanks 71

Day Two: Rejoice Always 75

Day Three: Fullness of Joy 79

Day Four: Triumphant Joy 83

Day Five: Blessing of Hope, Joy, & Peace 86

Day Six: The Consolation of Joy 89

Weekly Reflection 92

Weekly Renewal 93

The Goodness of God 94

Final Reflection 95

Final Renewal 96

About the Author 100

Extras 101

Reader Bonus 102

To all who mourn in Israel, he will give a crown of beauty for ashes, a joyous blessing instead of mourning, festive praise instead of despair. In their righteousness, they will be like great oaks that the LORD has planted for his own glory.

Isaiah 61:3 NLT

A Note from the Author

Childhood trauma often creates a disconnect between the survivor and God which can make the Christmas season difficult. Christmas often triggers survivors, leaving them feeling isolated in a world of celebration they cannot relate to.

As I share in my memoir, *What Kind of Love is This? Finding God in the Darkness*, I am a survivor of childhood trauma, I know the pain and uncertainty of reconciling complex emotions with the celebrations that surround Christmas.

Please take time each day to record your thoughts in the space provided. My prayer is you will find new wonder and hope not only during this season but throughout the year.

In Christ,

Charlotte B. Thomason

How to Use This Devotional

Light in the Darkness includes four weeks of daily devotionals, space for reflection, and a daily prayer. Each week concludes with space for weekly reflection. The weekly themes: hope, love, peace, and joy are often difficult concepts for trauma survivors to embrace. The addition of space for reflection and renewal allows the reader to dig deeper into these difficult aspects of life. Each day you will have opportunity to read, reflect, and renew.

READ

Set aside a specific time to read each day's devotional. Early morning or at bedtime work well for reading and reflecting.

REFLECT

Each devotional includes a question for reflection that challenges you to dig deeper. Write your thoughts in the space provided.

RENEW

Prayer may be difficult for you at first, so I've provided a suggested prayer for each day with space to add your personal thoughts.

Week 1: Hope

Many survivors get stuck in hopelessness especially during the holiday season, partially because the season often includes triggers of past trauma, but also because we struggle to believe our lives will ever be free from the aftermath of the trauma. As you prepare for Christmas this year, consider what hope means. According to the Oxford dictionary, "hope is a feeling of desire and expectation for something to happen."

Hope is a feeling, not something tangible, but a feeling. You can't touch it, wrap it up and put a bow on it, but you can experience it. Hope allows you to look toward the future rather than staying stuck in the past. Yes, doing so is difficult, especially in the beginning stages of healing from trauma, but the other two characteristics of hope provide clues to help you change your perspective from hopelessness to hope.

A feeling of desire and an expectation for something to happen opens the door to looking forward instead of backward. I met Jesus at a very young age and formed a close relationship with Him. While I didn't fully comprehend why He didn't stop the abuse I suffered, the connection with Him gave me hope that there was a possibility of something better and I knew I wanted to find it. Hope kept me alive and sane through the years of torment I endured.

The devotionals, reflections, and prayers in Week 1 offer six scriptures that address looking toward the future with hope.

"Hope is a feeling of desire and expectation for something to happen."

Day One: A New Thing

Read ✦

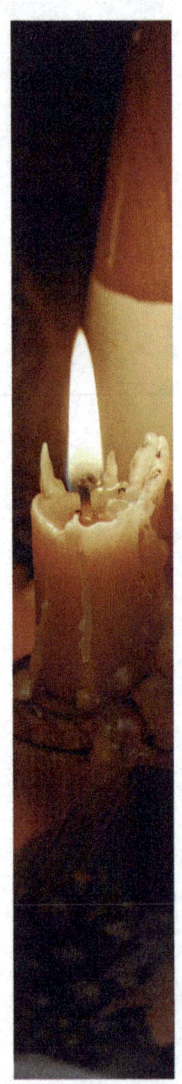

Forget the former things; do not dwell on the past. See, I am doing a new thing! Now it springs up; do you not perceive it? I am making a way in the wilderness and streams in the wasteland. Isaiah 43:18-19

Isaiah reminds us to keep our eyes forward. While I don't think he intends for us to forget the lessons from the past, his prophetic words stress the importance of seeing God at work even in desolate times.

Our vision gets clouded when we focus on missed opportunities, failures, or hardships from years gone by, which may cause us to miss the wonder that awaits us in the present. We cannot change the past, but we can look for evidence of God starting a new thing. He is watering the deserts, clearing the wilderness, and charting our course for whatever plans He has for us. We cannot see Him at work unless we keep moving forward.

> **We cannot change the past, but we can look for evidence of God starting a new thing.**

Date:

Reflect

Where do you see God working in your life?

Notes

Date:

Lord, please keep my eyes open to see the ways you are present in my life.

Notes

◆

Day Two: Keeper of your Soul

Read

The Lord will keep you from all evil; he will keep your life. The Lord will keep your going out and you're coming in from this time forth and forevermore. Psalm 121:7-8

The word "keep" is key to understanding today's passage. The Hebrew word is "samar," which means to guard, watch over or keep. The psalmist assures us that the Lord watches over us and guards us from evil every minute of every day.

Some might ask, "if God keeps us from evil, why do we suffer?" While the answer is more complicated than I can address here, today's verse establishes the promise of eternal protection for our souls. In other words, trials, pain, illness, and other tribulations will not have the final word. God will. He keeps watch and provides a haven through every storm we face.

> ...trials, pain, illness, and other tribulations will not have the final word. God will.

Date:

How is God watching over you?

Notes

✦

Date:

Lord, watch over me, guard my heart, mind, and soul.

Notes

Day Three: Patience in the Gap

Read ✦

Be strong, and let your heart take courage, all you who wait for the Lord! Psalm 31:24

Patience is a necessary aspect of hope. If you're like me, you want to be done with the heartache and pain of healing. Sometimes, you may think the process will always be difficult. You may become frustrated and disillusioned when faced with obstacles that cause delays, or you may encounter detours that seem to take you in an entirely different direction. Sometimes you stand at a crossroads where you face multiple choices that confuse us. What seemed clear at the beginning of the year suddenly seems impossible.

Today's verse reminds us to stand firm in the path God places on and patiently wait on His direction for each step we take. We must be courageous in the face of distractions and doubt and wait for Him to lead us.

Stand firm in the path God places on and patiently wait on His direction for each step we take.

Date:

How can you exercise more patience?

Notes

Date:

Lord, help me be patient as I wait for your guidance.

Notes

✦

Day Four: The Hidden Things
Read

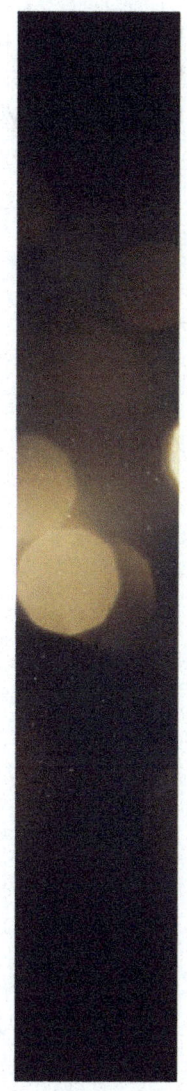

Call to me and I will answer you and will tell you great and hidden things that you have not known. Jeremiah 33:3

I read this verse several months ago and it reminded me how important prayer is to my relationship with the Lord.

Even though God is omnipotent and omnipresent, He wants to hear from us daily. He wants to reveal the "hidden things" to us. He wants to impart wisdom, comfort, and encouragement to us.

However, today's verse reminds us to call to him and He will answer. The answer may not come when or how we think it should, but it will come. Daily conversations with the Lord strengthen our ability to hear His voice and to discern whether our requests are made according to His will or according to what WE want. His desire is to bless us in every way and daily conversations with Him ensure our hearts and minds are open to receive them.

He wants to reveal the "hidden things" to us.

Date:

What "hidden things" has God revealed to you?

Notes

Date:

Lord, help me recognize the blessings you give me.

Notes

Day Five: Hope in Him

Read ✦

"The Lord is my portion," says my soul, "therefore I will hope in him." Lamentations 3:24

The word "portion" refers to an inheritance which indicates a legacy left to meet the needs of descendants. Today's verse assures us God will meet our needs because our inheritance is in Him through Christ.

We have no need to worry because God is our portion. Anxiety and doubt are driven away by the hope we have in our right standing with the Lord.

The word "portion" refers to inheritance.

Date:

According to today's verse, what is your portion?

Notes

✦

Date:

Lord, help me learn how to trust you.

Notes

◆

Day Six: I Hope in your Word
Read ✦

You are my hiding place and my shield. I hope in your Word. Psalm 119: 114

David's relationship with the Lord was profound and intimate. Reading Psalms gives us a glimpse of heaven as we listen to David's conversations with God.

David knew heartache and faced life threatening situations throughout his life and trusted God to see him through. In today's verse, David declares two essential qualities of God's character: shelter and protection.

Sometimes we need a safe place to hide for a season so we can be restored. God hides us in His arms when the circumstances around us are more than we can handle. He gives us a place to be with Him alone until we are strong enough to face the challenge.

The final phrase of the verse ties everything together. Although David did not know Jesus, he knew the importance of God's instruction. God's promises give us hope, protection, and shelter.

> . . . but they who wait for the LORD shall renew their strength;

Date:

What are some examples of time the Lord protected or hid you?

Notes

✦

Date:

What are some examples of time the Lord protected or hid you?

Notes

Date:

Weekly Reflection

What insights did you gain this week about hope?

Notes

Date:

Weekly Renewal

Use the space provided to have a conversation with God about hope.

Notes

Week 2: Love

As I held my beautiful newborn daughter for the first time, an unfamiliar feeling flowed over me. As tears rolled down my cheeks as I thought, "How can I ever give her the love she needs? I don't know what it feels like to be loved as I love her." As Korine opened her eyes, I prayed, "Lord what kind of love is this?" How do I show her this kind of love?" My greatest wish was to show my daughter the love I never received. I wanted her to feel the depth of love that I felt at that moment.

As I look back on the experience, I understand why I felt so lost when it came to showing love to anyone, even my child. To me, love meant abuse. Love meant pain, betrayal, and isolation. For much of Korine's childhood, I was a mess of depression and anxiety. As I journeyed through the darkness created by the abuse I endured as a child; I often could barely put one foot in front of another. I made mistakes. I felt helpless. Worry plagued me that I was a horrible mother. But during the chaos, somehow, Korine felt loved.

As the years passed, I constantly wondered: How could I love my daughter when I felt so unloved? How did I know about unconditional love? Sure, I considered the idea that the source was God, but I never completely believed He could love me or show me how to love someone else. I knew God loved my daughter but could not comprehend His love for me. I experienced intense emotions associated with what I thought was God's love, but seeds of doubt kept me from fully embracing the idea that God loved me. I had faith, but rationally, God's unconditional love eluded me.

The Greatest Gift

Eventually, I realized my story was common among survivors of childhood abuse. For many, scripture and faith may provide a level of healing. However, the idea that God could love them simply does not make sense, which makes accepting His love nearly impossible. While they can accept Christ and love God, many women need to understand how God could love them. Like me, they may believe that God loves others but struggle with being loved by Him. For some, associating the term love with God brings up fear and anger rather than peace and joy.

For a survivor who often views love as power, control, or pain, considering the alternative that God's love means that He wants only good for you may help you see God differently. He is not the father, uncle, cousin, or brother that abused you. His expression of love means He wants the best for you, with nothing expected in return. He does not want to control you but wants you to experience unconditional love. Just as I experienced incredible love for Korine the day I held her for the first time, God loves me simply because I exist. The knowledge helps me understand that the kind of love the Father has for me is the love of a Creator for His creation.

> **Just as I experienced incredible love for Korine the day I held her for the first time, God loves me simply because I exist.**

Day One: The Gift

Read

For by grace, you have been saved through faith. And this is not your own doing; it is the gift of God, not a result of works, so that no one may boast. Ephesians 2:8-9

For years I believed I had to earn God's love. I thought God was angry with me and desperately tried to prove I deserved His love.

The truth is God's love is an unconditional gift. Paul understood he couldn't earn redemption and spent years helping others understand God's gift to us through Jesus Christ.

We can't earn salvation. It is a gift. Grace was given to us while we were deep in sin. Christ died for all sin. We are redeemed by grace, not works. There is no performance-based entrance exam to heaven. The only requirement is accepting and fully embracing Jesus Christ as our savior and surrendering our life to Him.

> **There is no performance-based entrance exam to heaven.**

Date:

How have you seen God's unconditional love in your life?

Notes

✦

Date:

Lord, thank you for the gift of your Son. Help me understand the love you have for me.

Notes

Day Two: First Love
Read ◆

We love because He first loved us. 1 John 4:19

As I child I endured sexual, physical, and emotional abuse from multiple family members and others until I left home at age 18. The experiences left me with a distorted view of love and sex. To me, love meant power, control, and pain. In my mind, there was no distinction between love and sex. However, I also knew Jesus as my friend from a very young age. His presence gave me hope, but also confused me. How could He love someone like me? I didn't understand the kind of love I heard about in Sunday school until years later when someone demonstrated unconditional love to me.

Without understanding the unconditional love of Jesus Christ, we cannot fully comprehend love. He showed us what love can do. Love that transcends our human understanding comes only from the Father through His Son. Love like this transforms our perspective of everything and everyone we encounter. We see the world and ourselves differently when we are touched by the unconditional love of the Lord.

I didn't understand the kind of love I heard about in Sunday school until years later when someone demonstrated unconditional love to me.

Date:

Have you experienced unconditional love? Describe the experience in the space provided.

Notes

♦

Date:

Lord, I want to understand your unconditional love. How do I experience it after all I've been through?

Notes

Day Three: In this is Love
Read ✦

In this is love, not that we have loved God but that he loved us and sent his Son to be the propitiation for our sins. 1 John 4:10

Throughout the book of 1 John, we find the theme of love. John wants his audience to understand the enormity of the love God has for humanity. Today's verse captures the essence of love in one powerful sentence.

According to John, love is defined by what we receive more than by what we give. Receiving and accepting love frees us to give it to others. When we fully embrace God's unconditional love, our hearts are filled to overflowing to the point we cannot contain it. We can then give to others out of the abundance we receive.

Through Christ, we experience the fullness of God's love for us. As another verse reminds us, "we love because He first loved us."

When we fully embrace God's unconditional love, our hearts are filled to overflowing to the point we cannot contain it.

Date:

How do you define love? How does your definition compare to today's verse?

Notes

Date:

Lord, let me experience the love you have for me.

Notes

✦

Day Four: God So Loved Us

Read ✦

For God so loved the world, that he gave his only Son, that whoever believes in him should not perish but have eternal life. John 3:16

God desires a relationship with us. He wants to communicate with us daily, but that connection was severed when Adam and Eve chose to eat the fruit of the forbidden tree.

Humanity floundered for centuries and entered a cycle of sin-repentance-sin that led to slavery, destruction, and rigidity. Even when God delivered them, the Israelites rebelled, complained, and resisted God's sovereignty.

Communication with God came through the priests. Atonement was given through sacrifice of an animal. Ritual replaced personal communication. God sent His Son to redeem us and restore the personal connection between himself and His creation. He came to earth as a man to demonstrate His love for us. Through Christ, He brought us home. Through Christ, He removed the stain of the Garden once and for all. The veil of the temple was torn and our high priest, Jesus Christ, became our intercessor before God.

Through Christ, He removed the stain of the Garden once and for all.

Date:

How do you think God sees you? Does today's devotional change your view of yourself?

Notes

Date:

Lord, help me understand the gift of your Son.

Notes

Day Five: His Steadfast Love

Read ✦

Because your steadfast love is better than life, my lips will praise you. So, I will bless you as long as I live; in your name, I will lift up my hands. Psalm 63:3-4

When we first experience God's love in our core, we cannot contain it. Our heart explodes with indescribable joy. David's description, "your steadfast love is better than life," provides a clue to the exuberance felt when we embrace God's unconditional love. New life begins and the old is washed away.

It's difficult to contain the wonder and excitement of the moment we recognize all God is and all He does for us. David's response, "my lips will praise you . . . I will lift up my hands," reminds us to not withhold our joy.

The moment of awareness brings joy beyond description, but David reminds us of the importance of daily connection with the Lord. Daily renewal restores our soul. While we may not always feel like dancing in the streets with joy, our lips can praise Him as we lift our hands because "His steadfast love is better than life."

> **When we first experience God's love in our core, we cannot contain it. Our heart explodes with indescribable joy.**

Date:

When have you experience an awareness of God's love for you?

Notes

◆

Date:

Lord, thank you for loving me. I forget how much you love me sometimes. Help me remember.

Notes

✦

Day Six: Write it on your Heart

Read ◆

Let not steadfast love and faithfulness forsake you; bind them around your neck; write them on the tablet of your heart. So, you will find favor and good success in the sight of God and man. Proverbs 3:3-4

The visual presented in today's verse is dramatic. At first glance, the words, "Bind them around your neck," seem harsh and punitive. However, when we consider how easily we forget God's love and faithfulness when we encounter trials, "binding them" makes sense. Doing so means faith and love are secure no matter what we face.

"Write them on the tablet of your heart," is less severe, but requires action on our part. When I read these words, I think of conversations I've had with God throughout my life. Many were "written on my heart" and come to mind in times of darkness. Writing utilizes at least two senses: sight and touch. When we write our experience with God on our heart, we connect what we see with the touch of the Holy Spirit. Then in times of despair, the Holy Spirit reminds us of God's promises to us. In times of confusion, He leads us toward the finish line He has prepared for us. In times of joy, He cheers us on with reminders of all He has done.

When we write our experience with God on our heart, we connect what we see with the touch of the Holy Spirit.

Date:

How would you write God's steadfast love and faithfulness on the tablet of your heart?

Notes

Date:

Lord, help me remember to connect with you every day.

Notes

✦

Date:

Weekly Reflection

How did the Week Two devotionals affect your perspective about love?

Notes

Date:

Weekly Renewal

Use the space provided to have a conversation with God about love.

Notes

Week 3: Peace

Hurricanes are devastating and frightening. The path of the storm is unpredictable as is its strength as it travels across land and sea. While modern weather technology provides reliable predictions about a hurricane's path, the storms do not always follow the projection. However, every hurricane has an eye. The force of the surface winds deflects the wind slightly away from the center, causing the wind to rotate around the center of the hurricane, leaving the exact center, the eye, calm. While the storm's path and strength remain unpredictable, the eye remains constant and peaceful.

In Matthew 8: 23-27, the raging wind and torrential rain terrified these strong men, and they could not understand how Christ remained calm enough to sleep through the unyielding storm. Surely, they would die! Christ slept because He knew He was the calm center. He knew He could calm the sea. When the disciples doubted Christ's ability to divert the winds of the storm, He rebuked them. They lost their focus amidst a raging storm. They took their eyes off the calm center, Jesus.

The wind beat against their bodies and tore their clothes. The rain soaked them to the bone, leaving them cold and shivering. Once the wind was calm, they were still cold, shivering, and battered. However, in the aftermath, they were calm because

Rest for the Weary

Christ became their focus, rather than their circumstances.

At times life feels like a hurricane, tossing us to and fro with hurt, illness, unexpected changes, stress, anxiety, and challenging decisions. We become so caught up in the chaos that we cannot fathom relief. We may even cry out to God, "How can you let this happen to me?" All we see is the chaos. We do not see the peace available at the center. Christ stands at the center, like the eye of a hurricane, waiting for us to turn our eyes toward Him. He will take the brunt of the wind and rain. Even when the storm continues, He remains calm. When we focus on Him rather than the problems, confusion, or pain in our lives, we experience peace. Perhaps the circumstances do not change, but we change in the circumstances.

Then he got into the boat and his disciples followed him. 24 Suddenly a furious storm came up on the lake, so that the waves swept over the boat. But Jesus was sleeping. 25 The disciples went and woke him, saying, "Lord, save us! We're going to drown!"

26 He replied, "You of little faith, why are you so afraid?" Then he got up and rebuked the winds and the waves, and it was completely calm.

27 The men were amazed and asked, "What kind of man is this? Even the winds and the waves obey him!" Matthew 8:23-27.

Day One: No Fear
Read ✦

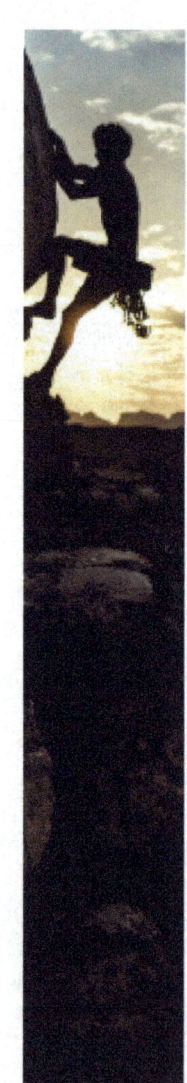

Peace, I leave with you; my peace I give to you. Not as the world gives do I give to you. Let not your hearts be troubled, neither let them be afraid. John 14:27

As we consider the current state of our world, peace seems like a distant memory or an impossible dream. Turmoil, violence, injustice, wars, and all manner of distress fill the news. It reminds me of a line from an old Christmas Carol, "there is no peace on earth."

The chaos around us often leads to depression and anxiety, but today's verse offers peace; not peace from the removal of the turmoil, but peace within our soul. The peace offered by Jesus calms our minds amid the most severe storm. We can cling to Him when the winds of chaos beat against us and threaten to topple our resolve. His presence quiets the storm within like nothing else can. As another song reminds us, "turn your eyes upon Jesus and the things of this world will grow strangely dim in the light of His glory and grace."

The peace offered by Jesus calms our mind amid the most severe storm.

Date:

When has Jesus calmed your mind during a storm?

Notes

✦

Date:

Renew

Lord, help me remember to keep my eyes on you and not the storm.

Notes

Day Two: Peace Beyond Measure

Read ◆

Do not be anxious about anything, but in everything by prayer and supplication with thanksgiving let your requests be made known to God. And the peace of God, which surpasses all understanding, will guard your hearts and your minds in Christ Jesus. Philippians 4:6-7

Today's passage is packed with insight and wisdom about tackling anxiety. Paul lays out a logical argument for putting worry to rest. First, he makes a declaration, "do not be anxious for anything." He continues with a roadmap for defeating anxiety. Finally, he declares the victory over worry that comes to those who follow the plan.

The middle step in the passage instructs us to submit our requests to the Lord, "by prayer and supplication with thanksgiving." All three elements are essential for the desired result. Prayer opens the line of communication. Supplication acknowledges God's sovereignty. Thanksgiving acknowledges faith in what we do not see.

The last phrase of the passage provides encouragement and hope. When we fully embrace God's unconditional love and petition Him with thanksgiving, He pours Himself out on us with indescribable peace. Peace that brightens every aspect of our being.

> All three elements are essential for the desired result. Prayer opens the line of communication. Supplication acknowledges God's sovereignty. Thanksgiving acknowledges faith in what we do not see.

Date:

What are your thoughts about approaching God with prayer, supplication, and thanksgiving?

Notes

✦

Date:

Renew

Lord, how can I find peace? Teach me how to prayer, submit, and be thankful.

Notes

Day Three: Peaceful Sleep
Read ✦

In peace I will both lie down and sleep; for you alone, O Lord, make me dwell in safety. Psalm 4:8

Trust in the Lord and peace go hand in hand. Anxiety and doubt flee when we trust God to keep us safe.

However, trust isn't easy for some because of their life experiences. A life of betrayal or hurt makes it difficult to trust anyone, let alone God. It takes patience and baby steps to let God in, but the relief that comes is profound. Peaceful rest and joy replace restless nights as we allow the Lord to remove doubt and fear.

Anxiety and doubt flee when we trust God to keep us safe.

Date:

Reflect

What thoughts keep you awake? What can you do to change your thoughts?

Notes

✦

Date:

Renew

What thoughts keep you awake? What can you do to change your thoughts?

Notes

♦

Day Four: Peace for the Nations

Read ✦

Glory to God in the highest, and on earth peace among those with whom he is pleased! Luke 2:14

As the Christmas season approaches, we turn our thoughts to the birth of our savior. Today's verse reminds us of the significance of the night God became flesh and dwelt among us.

The angelic pronouncement acknowledges Jesus's divine nature and His humanity. They praise God in the heavens while proclaiming peace to those who please God.

The second phrase points to Christ's purpose of reconnecting humanity to the Father. After the fall, we were cut off from direct connection to God and God wanted to restore the connection. The only way to do that was through the ultimate sacrifice of His Son. Once the connection was restored, humanity could once again experience the peace of the Lord's presence.

Because Jesus came to earth as an infant, walked among us, and died for us, we can have a personal relationship with the Lord. As our relationship with Him grows, so does the peace within our soul.

> **The angelic pronouncement acknowledges Jesus's divine nature and His humanity. They praise God in the heavens while proclaiming peace to those who please God.**

Date:

How can you strengthen your relationship with Jesus?

Notes

✦

Date:

Lord, sometimes I struggle to understand who you are in my life, but I desire the peace you promised when you came to earth.

Notes

Day Five: Blessed

Read

The Lord bless you and keep you; the Lord make his face to shine upon you and be gracious to you; the Lord lift up his countenance upon you and give you peace. Numbers 6:24-26

I love this blessing!

Today I want to focus on the last phrase, "the Lord lift up His countenance upon you and give you peace."

At first glance, the last phrase appears like the second, but they are vastly different in meaning. Countenance is not the same as the face. Rather, "face" refers to the physical face while "countenance" is the expression on the face that reveals the feelings of the entity.

While we do not actually see God's countenance, we experience His love for us. His countenance lifts us up and brings us peace. It is His countenance that pierces the depths of despair and shows us the way out of the darkness.

While we do not actually see God's countenance, we experience His love for us.

Date:

Reflect

When have you experienced something, you would describe as God lifting His countenance upon you?

Notes

✦

Date:

Lord, I long for the peace that comes when you lift your countenance upon me.

Notes

♦

Day Six: Perfect Peace

Read

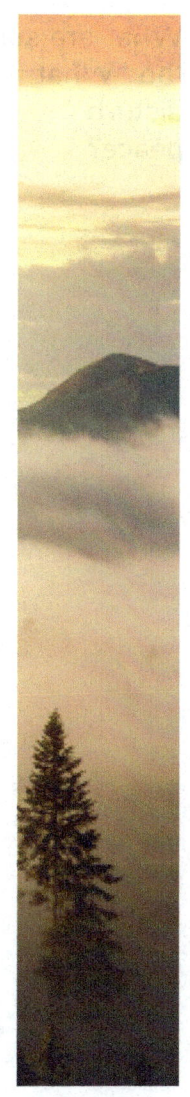

You keep him in perfect peace whose mind is stayed on you, because he trusts in you. Isaiah 26:3

The key phrase in today's verse is, "whose mind is stayed on you." Peace comes when our mind stays focused on the Lord. Our thoughts get jumbled, and we get distracted by the chaos of our current culture, but when we turn our eyes toward Jesus, the turmoil fades away and is replaced by peace.

When we get caught up in the "what ifs" of life, fear can replace peace, but when our mind is "stayed on" the Lord, the "what ifs" have no hold on us. They are fleeting thoughts that are quickly dismissed, and our peace is not disturbed.

Our thoughts get jumbled, and we get distracted by the chaos of our current culture, but when we turn our eyes toward Jesus, the turmoil fades away and is replaced by peace.

Date:

What are some of the "What ifs that disturb your peace?

Notes

✦

Date:

Lord, I want to keep my focus on you and not the chaos.

Notes

Date:

Weekly Reflection

What did you learn about peace from this week's devotionals?

Notes

Date:

Weekly Renewal

Have a conversa-tion with God about peace in the space provided.

Notes

Week 4: Joy

"Did you get it?", John asked with eager anticipation in his voice. "Yes, here it is," I replied, "Looks really good this year." "Should be, after the rain we had in January, he commented.

As he opened the pages of the magazine, he reminded me of a child who just opened the best Christmas present ever! For the next several hours, John poured over page after page of pictures of wildflowers. Nothing else mattered at that moment. I sat on the couch smiling each time he made an excited, "Wow! We need to go here this year!" Or "I know exactly where that is! I have a picture just like this one." By the end of the day, John had our route for our annual sojourn through the Texas Hill Country mapped out.

Every year we made the trip. It did not matter to John if we saw one bluebonnet or thousands. What mattered was the journey and ultimately seeing the result of God's workmanship throughout the winter. The bluebonnets peeked out from the grassy fields along the Texas highways like tiny beacons of light that illuminated the drab, colorless landscape of winter. Each blossom represented victory over the harshness of winter. Each blossom represented a new life and a new beginning.

I often wondered how these seemingly fragile plants bloom year after year. What miraculous events occur that result in such beauty? So, like any good 21st-century researcher, I Googled, "How to plant bluebonnets in Texas."

In short, to endure the winter, bluebonnets need to be planted in the right season, need sunlight, need contact and covering from the soil, need enough rain to soften their hard shell, and need to grow at their own pace with-

More Than Happiness

out being picked or rushed. As I read this, I was reminded that God works the same miracle with us every time we go through a severe (winter) season in our life.

Spring always follows winter. New life happens in every part of God's creation in the spring. Spring can be one of the most beautiful times of the year! However, when I am amid a difficult season in my life, I sometimes forget that spring is coming. I can't see any further than my circumstance. Fortunately, God knows SPRING IS COMING! I ask myself, why should I worry?

No matter how cold or dark the winters of your life seem, remember SPRING IS COMING! God provides all that you need to endure the winter. God's perfect plan will get you to spring.

As I read this, I was reminded that God works the same miracle with us every time we go through a severe (winter) season in our life.

Day One: Rejoice, Pray, Give Thanks

Read ◆

Rejoice always, pray without ceasing, give thanks in all circumstances; for this is the will of God in Christ Jesus for you. 1 Thessalonians 5:16-18

Paul begins the passage with, "Rejoice always," which some may find difficult to comprehend. Rejoicing in all circumstances contradicts our nature to reserve joy for celebrations and victories. However, Paul is most likely reminding us to never forget the joy planted in us by the Holy Spirit. Nothing can separate us from the joy in our soul.

Secondly, Paul tells us, "Pray without ceasing," which requires endurance. I don't think he intends for us to be uttering meaningless prayers all day, rather we should have a relationship with the Lord that allows us to have meaningful conversations with Him all day. Prayer is more than petitioning God; it is abiding in Him daily to strengthen our relationship with Him.

Paul's third declaration "give thanks in all circumstances," also gives us pause. How is it possible to give thanks when our life is torn apart by tragedy or setbacks? Paul's life and ministry provide an example of contentment in the worst of circumstances. He wrote most of his letters from prison. He doesn't say, "be thankful FOR all circumstances." Rather he says, "give thanks IN all circumstances." No matter what comes our way, we can be thankful for the unconditional love shown us through Christ Jesus.

> **Prayer is more than petitioning God; it is abiding in Him daily to strengthen our relationship with Him.**

Date:

What is the hardest part of today's verse for you to accept and why?

Notes

✦

Date:

Lord, how can I give thanks in all circumstances?

Notes

♦

Day Two: Rejoice Always
Read

Rejoice in the Lord always; again, I will say, rejoice. Philippians 4:4

Rejoicing in the Lord isn't always easy, especially in times of distress and grief. When we consider Paul's admonition in today's verse, we may wonder how we can always rejoice. To understand his intention, we must remember that joy and happiness are not the same thing. Paul is not saying, "always be happy." Unlike happiness, Joy is not dependent on outward circumstances, but is a condition of the soul.

Joy in the Lord comes when we acknowledge His presence in our hearts. When we turn our focus toward Him rather than our circumstances, we find contentment, comfort, and joy.

Paul tells his audience "Rejoice in the Lord," and then repeats the word "rejoice," as if he was aware of our tendency to lose focus in times of distress. The repetition reminds us that establishing new habits require consistent practice. If we practice rejoicing in the Lord regularly, our minds will automatically go to inner joy no matter what happens to us.

Joy in the Lord grounds us in truth. We can experience the intensity of grief, trials, and stress while maintaining inner joy because they are not mutually exclusive. A well-nourished seed of joy flourishes in all types of weather because it unaffected by external forces.

A well-nourished seed of joy flourishes in all types of weather because it unaffected by external forces.

Date:

What made you smile today?

Notes

♦

Date:

Lord, help me find the inner Joy that only comes from you.

Notes

Day Three: Fullness of Joy
Read ◆

These things I have spoken to you, that my joy may be in you, and that your joy may be full. John 15:11

The interesting thing about today's passage is Jesus's word choice. He doesn't say simply say He wants us to have joy, rather, He wants us to plant His joy in us. He continues by saying He wants our joy to be full. The Lord's words help us better understand the true nature of joy.

Jesus wants us to experience joy in all circumstances. While we will not always be happy, we can always find joy. Joy is the inner peace that comes from truly knowing Jesus. When we first experience Him in our innermost being, nothing compares to the joy of that moment. Words fail us when we attempt to describe the experience. No matter what happens in life, His joy remains in us. Sometimes we must dig deep to find it, but it is always there.

Fullness of joy comes through connection to Christ. In today's verse, Jesus explains why He's sharing His message, but it is up to us to listen to Him and build a relationship with Him. Without consistent connection, His joy might get buried under the stress and demands of the day. It's there, but difficult to access if we shift our focus off Him.

When our connection to Him is strong, we see Him, not the chaos around us. Just as Peter walked on water until he looked at the storm instead of Jesus, we can traverse any storm with joy by keeping our eyes on Jesus.

No matter what happens in life, His joy remains in us. Sometimes we must dig deep to find it, but it is always there.

Date:

How do you define Joy?

Notes

Date:

Lord, how do I shift my focus from the chaos to you?

Notes

Day Four: Triumphant Joy
Read ✦

Though the fig tree should not blossom, nor fruit be on the vines, the produce of the olive fails and the fields yield no food, the flock be cut off from the fold and there be no herd in the stalls, yet I will rejoice in the Lord; I will take joy in the God of my salvation. Habakkuk 3:17-18

A great reminder of the eternal nature of the joy we experience in the Lord.

The joy of the Lord is not dependent on our circumstances, rather it is the glue that holds our souls together in times of distress. Joy in the Lord survives loss, desolation, tragedy, disaster, and disappointment.

When all seems lost, the spark of joy planted in us by the Holy Spirit remains. Sometimes we must search our hearts to find it, but it's always there. Once we see it, faith ignites the spark and soon the flame illuminates the darkness. Joy overtakes sorrow and peace fills our souls.

Joy in the Lord survives loss, desolation, tragedy, disaster, and disappointment.

Date:

When have you experienced joy amid a tragedy?

Notes

✦

Date:

Lord, thank you for all the times you brought me joy when I couldn't see beyond the darkness.

Notes

✦

Day Five: Blessing of Hope, Joy, & Peace

Read

May the God of hope fill you with all joy and peace in believing, so that by the power of the Holy Spirit you may abound in hope. Romans 15:13

I love this blessing! It's a great way to begin the day. The verse addresses four essential aspects of life: hope, joy, peace, and faith.

Looking closer, I realized joy, peace, and faith are bookended by hope. The blessing begins with a petition to the Lord, the author of hope, to fill us with joy and peace, but is conditioned on faith. The verse ends with "that by the power of the Holy Spirit you may abound in hope." Paul doesn't say, "that you will have hope," but that we will abound in hope. The joy and peace will be so complete that we will jump for joy. We will not be able to contain it.

Hope begins when faith allows God to fill our souls and grows through the power of the Holy Spirit.

The joy and peace will be so complete that we will jump for joy. We will not be able to contain it.

Date:

Describe a time when you were so filled with joy that you couldn't help shouting, jumping, or expressing it in a demonstrative way.

Notes

◆

Date:

Lord, I want to experience the indescribable joy described in today's scripture.

Notes

Day Six: The Consolation of Joy

Read ✦

When the cares of my heart are many, your consolations cheer my soul. Psalm 94:19

Nothing lifts my soul like recalling the blessings I've received from the Lord. When grief, disappointment, or adversity threaten my peace, I find joy in His presence. I may still be sorrowful but have joy deep within my soul. Sorrow doesn't mean joy is gone. Rather, it's an opportunity to receive comfort from the Lord. Joy planted in my soul by the prince of peace will never fade.

He brings joy to the aching heart.

I may still be sorrowful but have joy deep within my soul.

Date:

When your heart is heavy, what brings you joy?

Notes

✦

Date:

Lord, help me experience joy when the cares of life weigh on my heart.

Notes

✦

Date:

Weekly Reflection

How did the Week Four Devotionals affect your perspective of joy?

Notes

Date:

Weekly Renewal

In the space provided, write a short prayer to God about joy.

Notes

Final Thoughts
The Goodness of God
Read

But for you who fear my name, the sun of righteousness shall rise with healing in its wings. You shall go out leaping like calves from the stall. Malachi 4:2

The righteousness of God shines on you with healing in its wings. You are getting stronger every day. God is restoring you. His love, comfort, and hope will empower you to burst from the stall and you will again frolic in the pasture He has prepared for you, and you will experience peace beyond your comprehension.

God is restoring you.

Date:

Final Reflection

What have you learned about the goodness of God over the last four weeks?

Notes

Final Renewal

Date:

What would you like to say to God today? What questions would you like Him to answer?

Notes

See what kind of love the Father has given to us, that we should be called children of God; and so we are.

1 John 3:1

About the Author

With a Master of Science in Social Work, a Master of Arts in Cultural Apologetics, over 30 years of experience in social work, and as a survivor of childhood trauma, Charlotte Thomason has seen, both professionally and personally, the devastation created by child abuse. She wants to use her experience to bring hope to those who feel lost and hopeless due to childhood trauma and bring encouragement to those who help them.

Other books by Charlotte B. Thomason

What Kind of Love is This? Finding God in the Darkness, (2020), Kharis Publishing.

Extras

Want to know more about the author of *Light in the Darkness*? Visit the link below for bonus features, multimedia, and updates on author signings and events.

https://efusionmg.com/extras/light-in-the-darkness

Reader Bonus

If you enjoyed *Light in the Darkness*, be sure to sign up for our VIP Reader Club for special offers, sneak peaks of new releases, and updates on special events.

Sign up below and receive a free digital book as a thank you.

https://efusionmg.com/vip/light-in-darkness

Made in the USA
Coppell, TX
21 August 2024

36306457R00066